Languages of the World

Arabic

Daniel Nunn

www.raintreepublishers.co.uk
Visit our website to find out
more information about
Raintree books.

To order:

☎ Phone 0845 6044371

🖹 Fax +44 (0) 1865 312263

🖳 Email myorders@raintreepublishers.co.uk

Customers from outside the UK please telephone +44 1865 312262

Raintree is an imprint of Capstone Global Library Limited,
a company incorporated in England and Wales having its
registered office at 7 Pilgrim Street, London, EC4V 6LB –
Registered company number: 6695582

Text © Capstone Global Library Limited 2012
First published in hardback in 2012
The moral rights of the proprietor have been asserted.

Edited by Dan Nunn and Diyan Leake
Designed by Marcus Bell
Original illustrations © Capstone Global Library Ltd 2012
Picture research by Elizabeth Alexander
Originated by Capstone Global Library Ltd
Printed and bound in China by South China Printing
  Company Ltd

ISBN 978 1 406 23282 0 (hardback)
15 14 13 12 11
10 9 8 7 6 5 4 3 2 1

British Library Cataloguing in Publication Data
Nunn, Daniel.
  Arabic. -- (Languages of the world)
  492.7-dc22
A full catalogue record for this book is available from the
British Library.

Acknowledgements
The author and publisher are grateful to the following
for permission to reproduce copyright material: Alamy
pp. 10 (© Gallo Images), 16 (© Image Source), 24 (© John
Warburton-Lee Photography); Corbis p. 28 (© Joshua
Dalsimer); Dreamstime.com p. 27 (© Vincent Giordano);
Getty Images pp. 17 (Alberto Coto/The Image Bank),
23 (Reza/Webistan); iStockphoto p. 14 (© Joel Carillet);
Photolibrary pp. 5 (Ron Giling), 6 (Bruno Barbier), 7
(Celia Peterson), 12 (Grapheast), 13 (Ron Giling), 15 (Peter
Widmann), 21 (Celia Peterson), 22 (Sean Sprague), 25 (Rafael
Macia), 29 (Imagesource); Shutterstock pp. 8 (© mtorrell),
9 left (© Tim UR), 9 right (© grekoff), 11 (© discpicture),
18 (© Mikael Damkier), 19 (© Seleznev Oleg), 20 (© Harald
Høiland Tjøstheim), 26 (© Elzbieta Sekowska).

Cover photograph reproduced with permission of Shutterstock
(© Monkey Business Images).

Every effort has been made to contact copyright holders of
material reproduced in this book. Any omissions will be
rectified in subsequent printings if notice is given to the
publisher.

Disclaimer
All the internet addresses (URLs) given in this book were valid
at the time of going to press. However, due to the dynamic
nature of the internet, some addresses may have changed, or
sites may have changed or ceased to exist since publication.
While the author and publisher regret any inconvenience this
may cause readers, no responsibility for any such changes can
be accepted by either the author or the publisher.

Contents

Arabic around the world 4

Spoken Arabic and Standard Arabic............................... 6

Arabic and English 8

Learning Arabic 10

Saying hello and goodbye... 12

Talking about yourself... 14

Asking about others... 16

At home 18

Families 20

At school.. 22

Sport 24

Food...26

Clothes...28

Pronunciation guide..30

Find out more 32

Index 32

Arabic words in this book are in italics, *like this*.
You can find out how to say them by looking in the
pronunciation guide.

Arabic around the world

Arabic is the main language of North Africa and the Middle East. It is spoken from Morocco in the west to the countries of the Arabian Peninsula in the east.

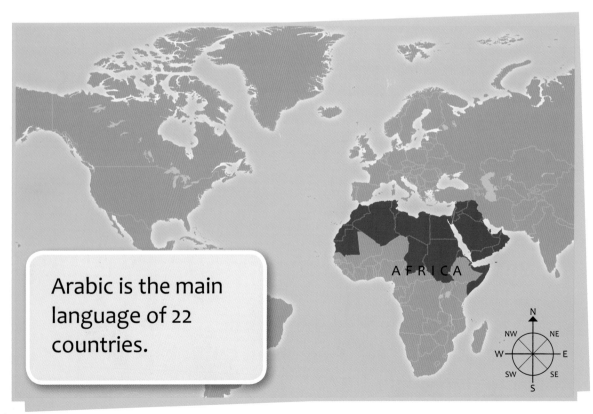

Arabic is the main language of 22 countries.

AFRICA

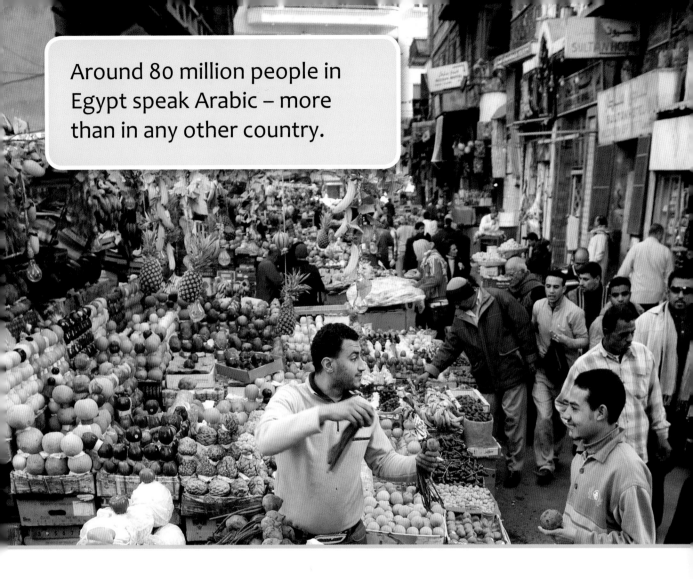

Around 80 million people in Egypt speak Arabic – more than in any other country.

Today, around 250 million people speak Arabic as their first language. Many Muslims around the world also know some Arabic. This is because Arabic is the language of the Qur'an, Islam's holy book.

Spoken Arabic and Standard Arabic

Spoken Arabic is the language spoken by ordinary people. Spoken Arabic is different from country to country. Someone from Morocco might not understand someone from Bahrain.

These Arabic speakers live in Morocco.

Arabic speakers from one country can use Standard Arabic to talk to people from other Arabic-speaking countries.

Standard Arabic is used in writing and on television and radio. Most Arabs understand it, no matter what country they are from. The Arabic in this book is Standard Arabic.

Arabic and English

Arabic is a very different language from English. It is not related to English like some other languages, such as German or French. It has its own alphabet. Some sounds in Arabic do not exist in English.

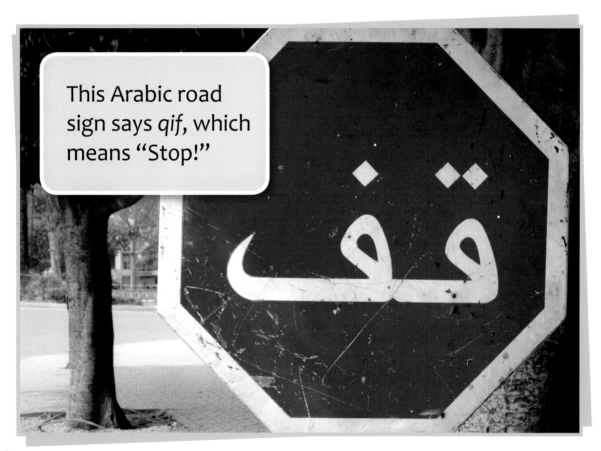

This Arabic road sign says *qif*, which means "Stop!"

The English words for fruits such as lemons, apricots, limes, and oranges all originally come from Arabic.

Even so, you may already know some Arabic words! Some of them have become part of the English language. The English words for coffee, giraffe, sugar, and jar all originally came from Arabic – *qahwa*, *zarāfa*, *sukkar*, and *jarra*.

Learning Arabic

The Arabic alphabet is very different from the alphabet used to write English. It is written from right to left. There are 28 letters in the Arabic alphabet.

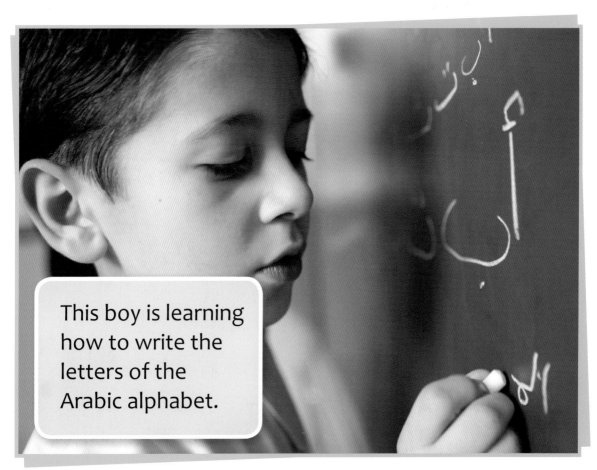

This boy is learning how to write the letters of the Arabic alphabet.

This picture shows the Arabic words for "book", "writer", and "library". Can you work out which are the letters k, t, and b?

كتاب
كاتب
مكتبة

Most words in Arabic are made from three main letters. For example, the letters k-t-b are used for words to do with writing. *Kitāb* means "book", *kātib* means "writer", and *maktaba* means "library".

Saying hello and goodbye

Arabs greet each other by saying, "*As-salām 'alaykum*", which means "Peace be upon you". The reply is usually "*Wa 'alaykum as-salām*", which means "And upon you, peace"!

How to say it
hello = *as-salām 'alaykum*
hello (in reply) = *wa 'alaykum as-salām*

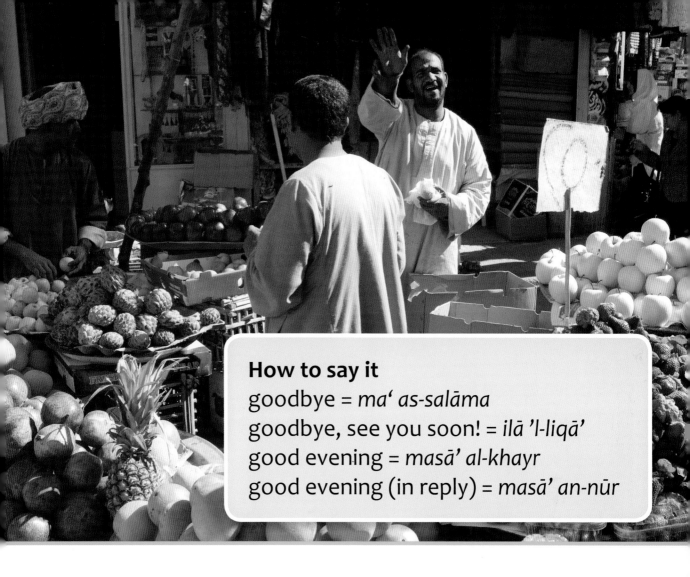

How to say it
goodbye = *ma' as-salāma*
goodbye, see you soon! = *ilā 'l-liqā'*
good evening = *masā' al-khayr*
good evening (in reply) = *masā' an-nūr*

To say goodbye, Arabs usually say, "*Ma' as-salāma*". You can also say, "*Ilā 'l-liqā'*" if you will see the person again soon. "Good evening" is *masā' al-khayr*, to which the reply is "*Masā' an-nūr*".

Talking about yourself

When you meet people for the first time, they may ask you what you are called. Then you can say, "*Ismī* ..." and then your name.

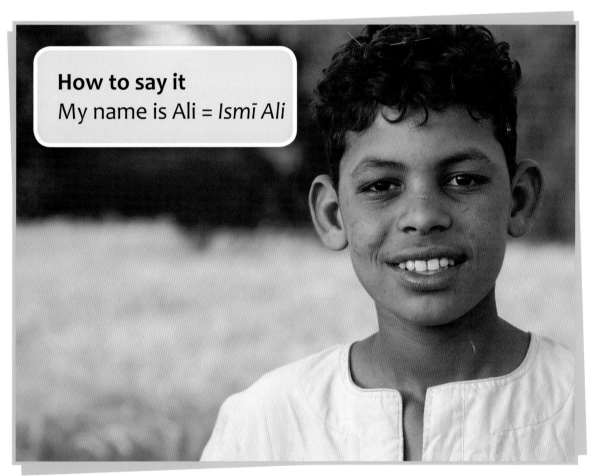

How to say it
My name is Ali = *Ismī Ali*

How to say it

Where are you from? = *Min ayna anta?*
  (to a boy)/*Min ayna anti?* (to a girl)
I'm from … = *Ana min …*
I live in = *Aysh fī …*

Then they might ask you where you are from. You can say, "*Ana min brīṭāniyā*" ("I am from Britain"). You can also say where you live: " *'Aysh fī landan*" ("I live in London").

Asking about others

It is usually polite to ask people about themselves. The first thing people might ask is someone's name. You can say, "*Mā ismak?*" to a boy or "*Mā ismik?*" to a girl.

How to say it
What is your name? = *Mā ismak?*/*Mā ismik?*

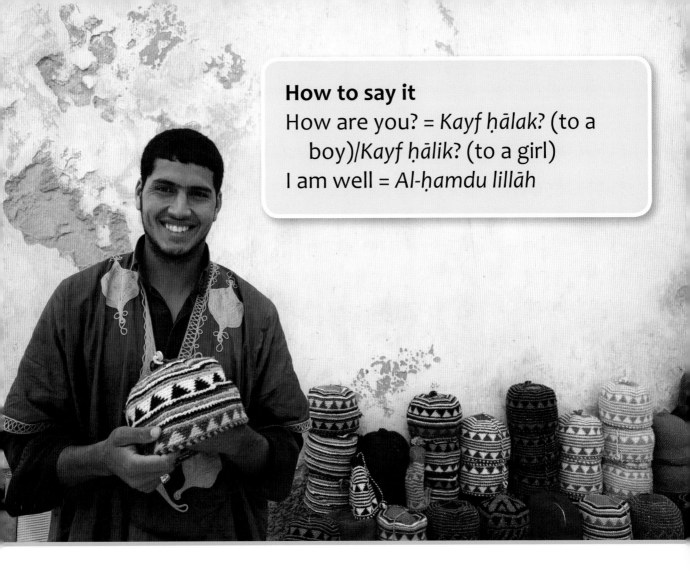

How to say it
How are you? = *Kayf ḥālak?* (to a
boy)/*Kayf ḥālik?* (to a girl)
I am well = *Al-ḥamdu lillāh*

To ask someone how they are, you say,
"*Kayf ḥālak/ḥālik?*" The answer is usually
"*Al-ḥamdu lillāh*". This means, "Praise
be to God", but people use it to mean,
"I am well".

At home

People's homes across the Arab world can be very different. Big cities such as Cairo and Damascus are very crowded. Most people live in flats. Some people even live on the roofs of large buildings.

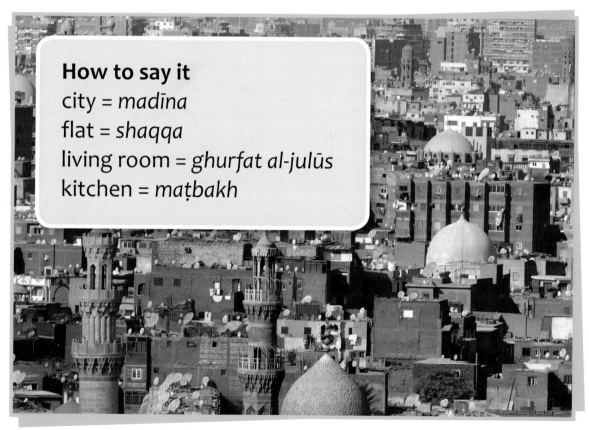

How to say it
city = *madīna*
flat = *shaqqa*
living room = *ghurfat al-julūs*
kitchen = *maṭbakh*

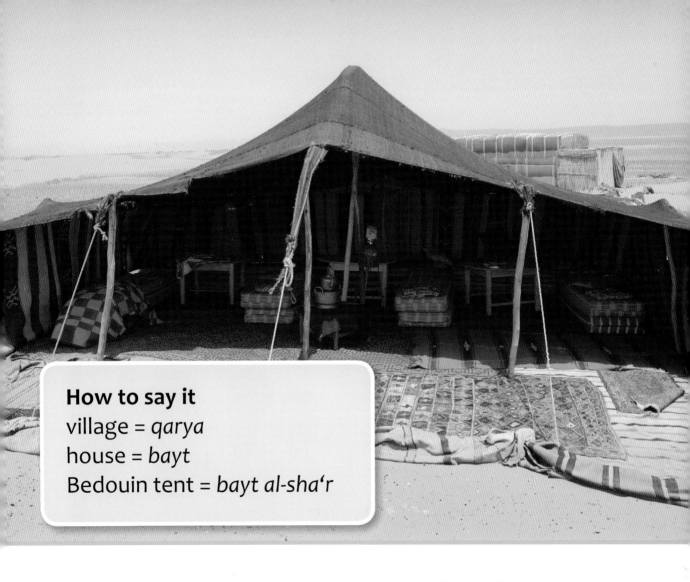

How to say it
village = *qarya*
house = *bayt*
Bedouin tent = *bayt al-sha'r*

In the countryside, people often live in villages. Village homes are usually small and simple. Some Bedouin Arabs live in tents. They call these *bayt al-sha'r*, which means "house of hair"!

Families

Families in many parts of the Arab world are quite large. Parents and children, aunts, uncles, cousins, and grandparents may all live close together or even share a house.

How to say it
grandmother = *jadda*
grandfather = *jadd*
aunt = *'amma* or *khāla*
uncle = *'amm* or *khāl*

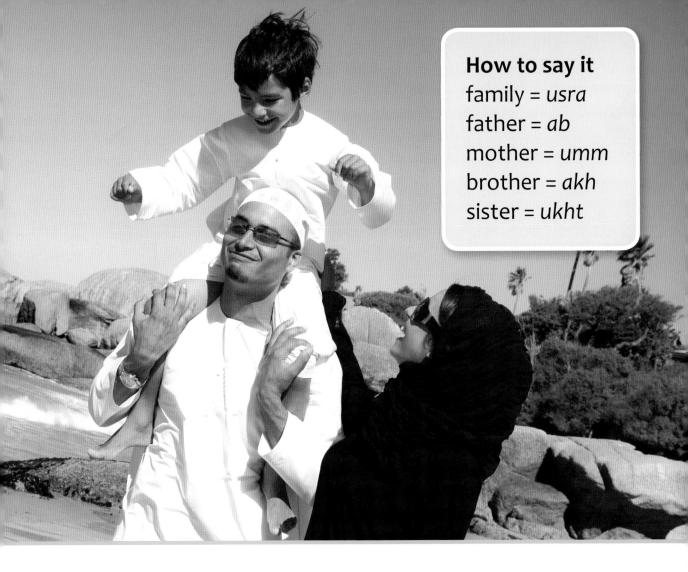

How to say it
family = *usra*
father = *ab*
mother = *umm*
brother = *akh*
sister = *ukht*

Parents take on the name of their oldest son, or daughter if they have no son. So, if they have a boy called Mazen, they become known as *Abū Mazen* ("Mazen's Father") and *Umm Mazen* ("Mazen's Mother").

At school

In most Arab countries, children go to school from Sunday to Thursday. At primary school, boys and girls are taught together. When they get older, they go to separate boys' and girls' schools.

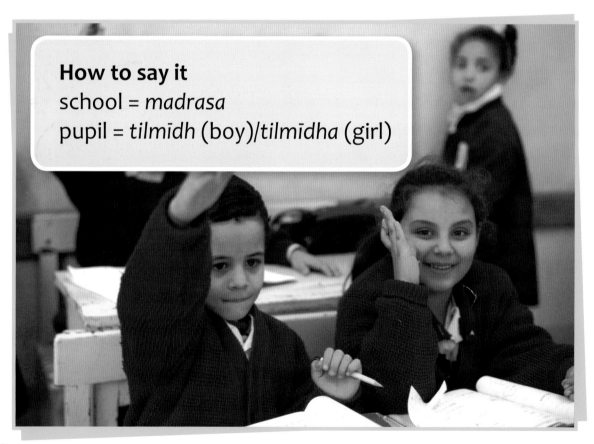

How to say it
school = *madrasa*
pupil = *tilmīdh* (boy)/*tilmīdha* (girl)

How to say it
maths = *riyāḍīyāt*
sciences = *'ulum*
English = *al-lugha al-inglīzīa*
Arabic = *al-lugha al-'arabīa*

Arab children learn lots of subjects at school – just like you! They study maths, sciences, geography, history, English or French, art, and music. They also learn how to read and write Standard Arabic.

Sport

Football is very popular in most Arab countries. In Egypt the two biggest teams are Ahly and Zamalek. Other popular sports are basketball, squash, and tennis.

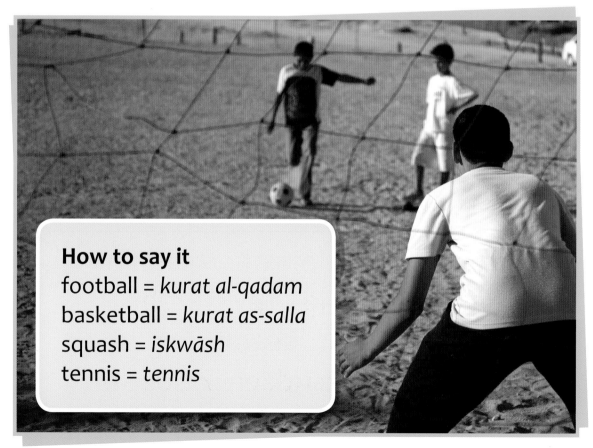

How to say it
football = *kurat al-qadam*
basketball = *kurat as-salla*
squash = *iskwāsh*
tennis = *tennis*

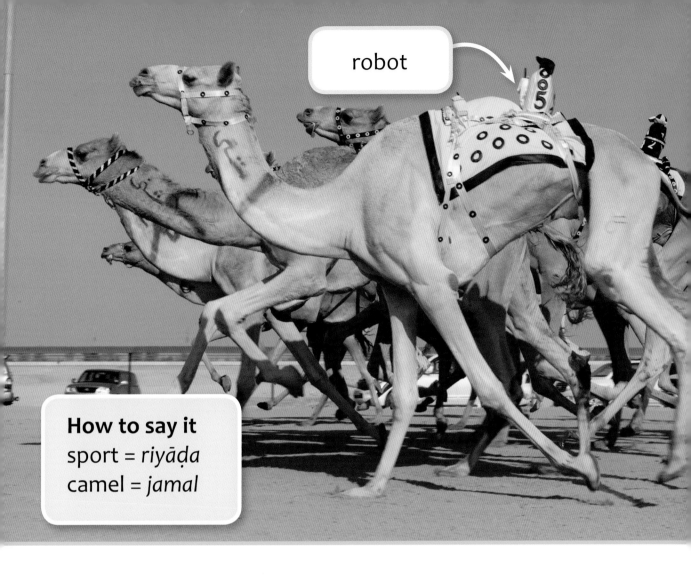

Camel racing is a popular sport in countries such as the United Arab Emirates and Qatar. In some races, the camels are even ridden by robots instead of people!

25

Food

Lamb and chicken dishes served with rice are popular across the Arab world. One famous dish from Morocco is the tagine, a meaty stew cooked in a special pot.

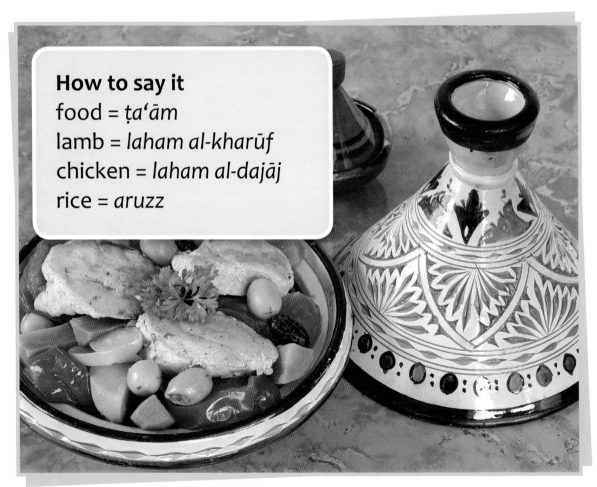

How to say it
food = ṭaʿām
lamb = *laham al-kharūf*
chicken = *laham al-dajāj*
rice = *aruzz*

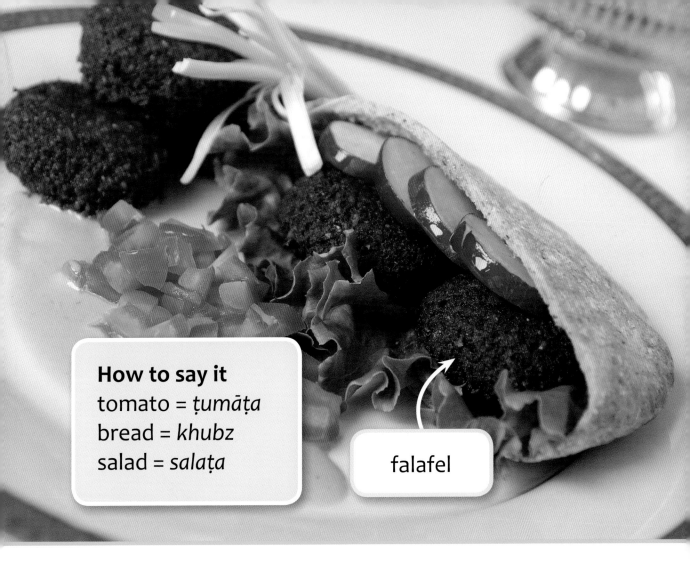

How to say it
tomato = *ṭumāṭa*
bread = *khubz*
salad = *salaṭa*

falafel

The most famous Arab food is from Lebanon. There are Lebanese restaurants all over the world. Popular Lebanese food includes bread dipped in hummus, falafel, and pastries filled with chopped nuts.

Clothes

In countries such as Egypt, some people wear Western-style clothing and some people wear traditional Arab clothes. Many women wear headscarves called *ḥijab*, but some women do not.

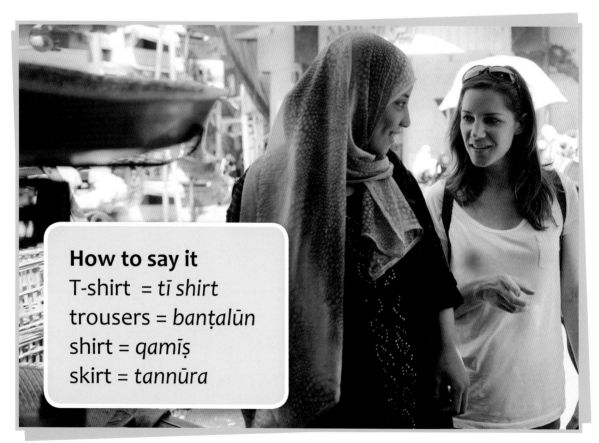

How to say it
T-shirt = *tī shirt*
trousers = *banṭalūn*
shirt = *qamīṣ*
skirt = *tannūra*

This man and the boys are wearing a *dishdash*. The woman is wearing an *abaya*. These clothes are the national dress of the United Arab Emirates.

In countries such as the United Arab Emirates and Saudi Arabia, most people wear traditional Arab clothes. Men wear a long white robe called a *dishdash*. Women wear a long cloak called an *abaya*.

Pronunciation guide

English	Arabic	Pronunciation
apartment	*shaqqa*	**shaq**-qa
Arabic	*al-lugha al-'arabīa*	al-**lu**-rra al-ara-**bee**-a
aunt	*'amma* or *khāla*	**am**-ma / **khaa**-la
basketball	*kurat as-salla*	**ku**-rat as-**sal**-la
Bedouin tent	*bayt al-sha'r*	**bayt** ash-**sha**-ar
book	*kitāb*	ki-**taab**
bread	*khubz*	**khubz**
brother	*akh*	**akh**
camel	*jamal*	**ja**-mal
chicken	*laham al-dajāj*	**la**-ham ad-da-**daaj**
city	*madīna*	ma-**dee**-na
English	*al-lugha al-inglīzīa*	al-**lu**-rra al-ing-lee-**zee**-a
family	*usra*	**us**-ra
father	*ab*	**ab**
food	*ṭa'ām*	ta-**aam**
football	*kurat al-qadam*	**ku**-rat al-**qa**-dam
giraffe	*zarāfa*	za-**raa**-fa
good evening	*masā' al-khayr*	ma-**saa** al-**khayr**
good evening (in reply)	*masā' an-nūr*	ma-**saa** an-**noor**
goodbye	*ma' as-salāma*	**ma**-a as-sa-**laa**-ma
goodbye, see you soon	*ilā l-liqā'*	i-**laa** li-**qaa**-a
grandfather	*jadd*	**jadd**
grandmother	*jadda*	**jad**-da
hello	*as-salām 'alaykum*	as-sa-**laam** a-**lay**-kum
hello (in reply)	*wa 'alaykum as-salām*	wa a-**lay**-kum as-sa-**laam**
house	*bayt*	**bayt**
How are you?	*Kayf ḥālak?* (to a boy)	**kayf haa**-lak
	Kayf ḥālik? (to a girl)	**kayf haa**-lik

I am well	Al-ḥamdu lillāh	al-**ham**-dul lil-**laa**
I live in ...	Aysh fī ...	**aysh fee**
I'm from ...	Ana min ...	**a**-na **min**
jar	jarra	**jar**-ra
kitchen	maṭbakh	**mat**-bakh
lamb	laham al-kharūf	**la**-ham al-kha-**roof**
library	maktaba	**mak**-ta-ba
living room	ghurfat al-julūs	**rrur**-fat al-ju-**loos**
maths	riyāḍīyāt	ri-yaa-dee-**yaat**
mother	umm	**umm**
My name is ...	Ismī ...	is-**mee**
pupil	tilmīdh (boy)/tilmīdha (girl)	til-**meeth** / til-**mee**-tha
rice	aruzz	a-**ruz**
salad	salaṭa	**sa**-la-ta
school	madrasa	**mad**-ra-sa
sciences	'ulum	**u**-lum
shirt	qamīṣ	qa-**mees**
sister	ukht	**ukht**
skirt	tannūra	tan-**noo**-ra
sport	riyāḍa	ri-**yaa**-da
squash	iskwāsh	is-**kwaash**
sugar	sukkar	**suk**-kar
T-shirt	tī shirt	**tee**-shirt
tennis	tennis	**ten**-nis
tomato	tumāta	tu-**maa**-ta
trousers	banṭalūn	ban-ta-**loon**
uncle	'amm or khāl	**amm** or **khaal**
village	qarya	qa-**ree**-ya
What is your name?	Mā ismak? (to a boy)	**maa is**-mak
	Mā ismik? (to a girl)	**maa is**-mik
Where are you from?	Min ayna anta? (to a boy)	**min ay**-na **an**-ta
	Min ayna anti? (to a girl)	**min ay**-na **an**-ti
writer	kātib	**kaa**-tib

Find out more

Books

My First Book of Arabic Words, Katy R. Kudela (Capstone, 2011)
A Visit to Egypt, Peter and Connie Roop (Heinemann
    Library, 2008)

Website

Learn all about the Arabic alphabet at www.funwitharabic.com.

Index

Arabian Peninsula 4
Bahrain 6
Bedouin Arabs 19
Egypt 5, 16 (Cairo), 24, 28
Lebanon 27
Morocco 4, 6, 8
Qatar 25
Saudi Arabia 29
Syria 18 (Damascus)
United Arab Emirates 25, 29